RAIN FORESTS IN DANGER

Sally Morgan

SEA-TO-SEA

Mankato Collingwood London

This edition first published in 2010 by
Sea-to-Sea Publications
Distributed by Black Rabbit Books
P.O. Box 3263, Mankato, Minnesota 56002

Printed in USA

Library of Congress Cataloging-in-Publication Data

Morgan, Sally.
  Rain forests in danger / Sally Morgan.
     p. cm. -- (Earth SOS)
  Includes index.
  ISBN 978-1-59771-225-5 (hardcover)
  1. Rain forests--Juvenile literature. 2. Rain forest conservation--
Juvenile literature. I. Title.
  QH86.M657 2010
  577.34--dc22
                                    2008053170

  9 8 7 6 5 4 3 2

Published by arrangement with the Watts
Publishing Group Ltd., London.

EARTH SOS is based on the series *EarthWatch* published by Franklin Watts.
It was produced for Franklin Watts by Bender Richardson White,
P O Box 266, Uxbridge UB9 5NX.
Project Editor: Lionel Bender
Text Editor: Jenny Vaughan
Original text adapted and updated by: Jenny Vaughan
Designer: Ben White
Picture Researchers: Cathy Stastny and Daniela Marceddu
Media Conversion and Make-up: Mike Weintroub, MW Graphics,
and Clare Oliver
Production: Kim Richardson

Picture Credits: Oxford Scientific Films: cover small photo & page 4 top
(Michael Fogden), 6 top (Martyn Colbeck), 10 (Frank Schneidermeyer),
11 bottom (Nick Gordon), 12 (Edward Parker), 13 top (M.
Wendler/Okapia), 18 (Daniel J. Cox), 19 bottom (Stan Osolinski), 26
(Daniel J. Cox). The Stock Market Photo Agency Inc.: cover main photo,
globe & pages 1, 6–7, 8, 17, 19 top, 22–23 (J. M. Roberts), 28. Ecoscene:
pages 4 bottom (Andrew Brown), 9 (Simon Grove), 14 (Alexandra Jones),
15 (Joel Creed), 27 top (Joel Creed). Panos Pictures: pages 11 top
(Arabella Cecil), 13 bottom (Ron Giling), 16 (J. Hartley), 20 (Chris
Stowers), 21 top (David Reed), 21 bottom (Jeremy Horner), 22 bottom
(Fred Hoogervorst), 24 (Liba Taylor), 25 bottom (Jean-Léo Dugast), 27
bottom (Arabella Cecil), 29 top (Fred Hoogervorst). Environmental
Images: pages 17 top (Mark Fallander), 25 top (Irene R. Lengui), 29
bottom (Herbert Girardet). Science Photo Library, London: pages 23
(Peter Menzel).

Artwork: Raymond Turvey.

Note to parents and teachers: Every effort has been made by the publisher to ensure that websites listed are suitable for children, that they are of the highest educational value, and that they contain no inappropriate or offensive material. However, because of the nature of the Internet, it is impossible to guarantee that the contents of these sites will not be altered. We strongly advise that Internet access is supervised by a responsible adult.

CONTENTS

RAIN FORESTS

Rain forests are a special kind of forest. They grow in warm, wet places. The trees are tall, and grow close together.

This tree frog lives in tropical forests in South America.

Tropical forests

Tropical rain forests grow near the **equator** (the middle of the Earth). The **climate** where they grow is hot, with a lot of rain. The biggest rain forest is around the **Amazon** River, in South America.

Cloud forests

There are rain forests high in the mountains near the equator. We call these forests cloud forests, because they are up in the clouds. The climate is cooler here, but very wet.

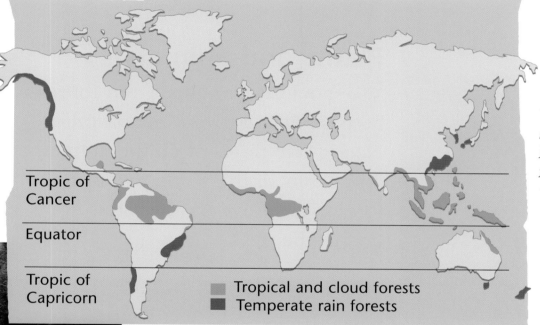

Tropic of Cancer

Equator

Tropic of Capricorn

Tropical and cloud forests
Temperate rain forests

This map shows the largest rain forests in the world.

This rain forest is on the island of Saint Lucia in the Caribbean, near the USA.

Temperate forests

Temperate rain forests grow farther from the equator. The climate here is cooler, and some parts of the year are quite cold. The trees here are often covered with thick moss, and plants called **lichens**. Many of the trees are **conifers**, such as fir and pine trees.

FORESTS AT RISK

We often see pictures of fires in rain forests. We also hear about people chopping down forests to make farms. Why should we worry about this?

Plants and animals

We should worry about rain forests, because they are very important. Nearly two-thirds of all the animals and plants in the world live in rain forests. They live on the forest floor, and in the trees.

People may burn forests to clear land for farming. Small fires do not do much harm.

Water travels up the trunk to the leaves. It evaporates out of the leaves.

HOW A TREE TAKES UP AND LOSES WATER

Water flows upward.

Leaves fall and rot. They are good for the soil.

Water passes into the tree through the roots.

These trees, ferns, and mosses are in a temperate rain forest in the USA.

Trees and rain

Forests are important because they affect the climate and weather. Trees take water from the ground. It reaches their leaves, and **evaporates**. This means it becomes a gas called **water vapor**. This rises into the air and forms rain clouds.

Gases in the air

Tree leaves make their own food from sunlight, water, and **carbon dioxide** gas in the air. This process gives off **oxygen** gas. Most living things need oxygen.

Eco Thought

In only 2.3 square miles (6 sq km) of rain forest, there can be more than 1,500 different kinds of flowering plants.

IN A RAIN FOREST

A rain forest is like a building, with many floors. Different plants and animals live on each floor.

Canopy

The top part of the forest is called the **canopy**. It is like the roof of the forest. Some trees are more than 130ft (40m) tall. Birds and monkeys live in these high branches.

Understory

The **understory** is under the canopy. Plants such as orchids grow on the tree bark. Creepers hang from the trees.

This is a canopy of a rain forest in Australia.

CANOPY

UNDERSTORY

Forest floor

Very little light gets through the leaves to the forest floor. It is too dark there for large plants to grow. It is often wet and warm, so leaves and twigs rot quickly. **Fungi** break down the leaves and produce substances that help plants to grow.

Eco Thought

In Central America, some forests are very thick. Monkeys can travel more than 37 miles (60km) without ever leaving the treetops.

FOREST
FLOOR

Heavy rain makes this forest floor muddy.

9

RAIN FOREST PEOPLE

People have been living in rain forests for thousands of years. They get everything they need from the forest.

These forest people in Papua New Guinea are getting ready for a feast.

Forest gardens

Rain forest people clear away small parts of the forest to make gardens. They grow plants they can use for food and medicines. Later, they leave the gardens, and make new ones. The old gardens soon become forest again. That way, the forest is not harmed.

On the Ground

In Brazil, one-quarter of the forest near the Amazon River is protected. Only forest people may live there.

Forest people get food by hunting and fishing.

The future

Rain forest people hunt animals and catch fish. But they never kill too many animals, or chop down too many trees. They only take what they need. But now rich farmers are taking over the forest. They clear land to grow huge fields of crops. Forest people have to leave.

This is a hunter in South America. He kills animals with a blowpipe and poison darts.

11

VANISHING FORESTS

Nearly 80 percent of the world's forests have gone. The rain forest around the Amazon may disappear in 100 years.

Clearing forest in Africa to make a small farm.

Land for farming

In Central and South America, rich farmers own the best land outside the forest. They have also cut down forests to make huge cattle farms. Poorer farmers cut down forests to grow food for themselves.

Eco Thought

In 1950, there were about 250 billion acres (1 billion hectares) of rain forest in the world. Soon, there may only be half as much left.

Wood

Companies that sell wood chop down the trees in rain forests. They use big machines to carry the trees away. They sell the wood to other countries where it is used to make furniture and houses. Thousands of acres of forest are destroyed.

Machines that are used to move logs can harm the forest.

Big business

Often huge parts of forests are burned, so that farmers can grow crops such as coffee and rubber. We call these **cash crops**, because they are crops for sale, not for food. Factories, mines, and dams may be built in forests. There is less land left for poor people.

These rubber trees are growing on land that used to be forest.

WASHED AWAY

Around 6in (15cm) of rain can fall in a day in some rain forests. That is six times as much as Los Angeles gets in some months.

A huge sponge

The rain forest is like a huge sponge. The plants soak up rainwater. It evaporates from the leaves. The water vapor forms clouds, and rain falls from the clouds to the forest below. Some water drains out of the forest soil and into rivers.

Water from the trees forms clouds and later falls as rain.

Water drains into rivers.

A TROPICAL RAIN FOREST

A waterfall in a tropical rain forest in Australia.

Erosion

Tree roots hold the soil. When people clear trees away, rain washes soil into rivers. Water animals and plants cannot live in the muddy water. They die.

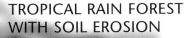

On the Ground

In Honduras, when people clear land, they use fast-growing plants to hold the soil. Later, they grow crops there.

Without the trees, rains wash away the soil. Mud fills the rivers.

Less rain

With fewer trees, the water runs away more quickly. Less water evaporates, so there is less rain. The climate of the forest changes.

*When rain washes soil away, **gulleys** (deep cracks) like this may form.*

15

THE CLIMATE

Rain forests give off huge amounts of water vapor. This affects the rain that falls all over the world.

Spreading rain

The Sun warms the rain forests. Water vapor rises into the air. It cools and changes to clouds. Wind blows these far from the forests. Without forests, other places may not get the rain they need.

When a forest is chopped down, the land may become dead and dry.

Try this

Put a saucer of water in a dry, sunny place like a windowsill. Leave it for a few days. What happens to the water? Why?

Global warming

When we burn wood, coal, gas, or oil, this gives off a gas called carbon dioxide. It traps heat from the Sun. If there is too much carbon dioxide, the climate gets too hot. This is called **global warming**. Trees use up carbon dioxide, so global warming gets worse if we destroy the forests.

These people are wearing masks so they do not breathe in smoke from burning rain forests.

Eco Thought

Forty years ago, there were big forests in Ethiopia, in Africa. Now the trees have gone, and the climate is drier.

In Malawi, in Africa, this forest has been cleared to grow tea. The climate in the area is now drier.

FOREST WILDLIFE

Living things need each other. For example, plants need animals to spread seeds, and animals eat plants. If one living thing dies, others may die, too.

Mountain gorillas need rain forests for food and as a place to live.

Under threat

Many plants and animals are dying out because rain forests are disappearing. For example, gorillas live in the forests of central Africa. The forests are being chopped down, so the gorillas may have nowhere to live, and no food. The gorillas may become **extinct**.

Eco Thought
Fifty kinds of rain forest animals die out each day.

Tigers live in the rain forests in Asia. There are only about 5,000 left in the world, because so many have been hunted, and so much forest has gone.

Forest strips

Big animals like tigers need a lot of land to hunt for food. When people destroy forests, animals get trapped in small areas. It is like being on an island. One way to help is to link these areas with strips of forest.
Animals can travel along the strips to new areas, to find food, and other animals.

Many kinds of parrots are dying out. These hyacinth macaws are in a zoo. Zoos can help save animals like these.

19

USING FORESTS

There are many things we can use in the forest. For example, some wood is used for building and for making furniture. This is called timber.

Logs from a rain forest floating down a river in Borneo, South-east Asia.

Logging

Cutting down trees in forests for their wood is called **logging**. Loggers damage forests as they cut down trees such as **hardwood** trees for **timber**.

Timber

The hardwood is sold to countries far away to make furniture. Local people make very little money from the wood. But the people who sell it make a lot of money.

Eco Thought
Logging damages forests badly. It takes many years for the trees to grow again.

This is a mine in Guinea, in Africa. It has damaged the forest.

These people in South America are digging for gold.

Mining

Mining companies clear away the forest. They dig into the ground, so they can look for metals. They dump waste on the land. Water carries the waste or **pollution** from this into rivers. Fish and other animals die.

Try this

Look at the furniture in your home. How many different kinds of wood can you find?

NEW FINDS

About half of all the different kinds of plants and animals in the world live in the rain forests. But scientists think they have only studied one-tenth of them.

New medicines

Long ago, forest people found that many forest plants can be used as medicines. About one-quarter of medicines we use today were first found in forests. Scientists think there may be many more.

Eco Thought

More than 2,000 rain forest plants could help fight diseases like cancer.

These students are learning about rain forest plants.

Forest foods

There are around 75,000 rain forest plants that we could eat. These include rice, coffee, and bananas. There must be many more, but we have not discovered them yet.

Discoveries

Scientists are always discovering new forest plants. They have found new fruits, and plants that contain substances that kill insects. One tree makes an oil we can use as fuel. If we lose the rain forests, we will never know how many useful plants there were.

A scientist studies a rain forest plant.

More than 30 different kinds of plants grow in the understory of this rain forest.

Try this

Plant an avocado stone in damp potting soil and keep it in a warm place. Water it regularly. What happens?

FOREST CARE

We must look after the rain forests, so that they are still there in the future. We can find ways of using the forests, but keeping them, too.

Careful cutting

In some places, small parts of the forest are cut down, and new trees are planted in their place. These are **sustainable forests**. In India and Central America, people plant trees that grow fast. They can be cut down again in 20 years.

Checking the number of logs on a truck in the rain forest.

Replanting trees

We can replant forests. But it takes a long time for new trees to grow. It takes even longer before new forests have as much wildlife as the old ones. But new forests are better than no forests.

These students in the Philippines are learning how to plant young trees.

This wood comes from a sustainable forest in Thailand.

Loggers' logo

A group called the Forest Stewardship Council checks if timber companies are caring for the forests they cut wood in. If they are, they can put the Council logo on the wood they sell.

Try this

Look at tropical timber for sale. Does it have "FSC" stamped on it? This stands for Forest Stewardship Council.

SAVING FORESTS

Forests are disappearing all the time. It is important for us to act fast to save them.

Protected parks

One way to save a rain forest is to turn it into a **national park** or a **nature reserve**. This protects the forest from loggers and farmers.

Eco-tourists

Rain forest people need money. **Eco-tourism** can bring this. This is tourism that does not harm the environment. Only a few tourists at a time visit the forest. They learn about the forest and do not damage it while they are there.

Eco Thought
In Central America, at least five new parks or nature reserves are set up every year.

Young orangutans in Malaysia. Local people can get jobs looking after animals like these.

Involving people

Cutting down trees and selling timber is a quick way of making money. But many rain forest people now want to use the rain forest to make money without harming it. That way, they can have money in the future as well as now.

Eco-tourists travel along a river in the Iguacu National Park in Brazil.

These forest people are making pottery to sell to tourists.

27

WHAT CAN WE DO?

Rain forests are important to everyone.
People and governments must work
together to save them.

World meeting

In 2002, there was a
meeting in South Africa.
It was called the World
Summit on Sustainable
Development. Experts,
politicians, and people
from all over the world
talked about how to save
rain forests.

Eco Thought

Around 300 million people
depend on rain forests.
They use the plants and
wood that grow there.

*Visitors should
stay on forest
paths, so they will
not damage plants.*

Children in Uganda, Africa, are growing trees for the rain forest.

A tree sculpture made for a meeting about the environment in Brazil in 1992.

Charities

Some charities work to protect the people of the rain forests, and the plants and animals that live there. We can help by giving money to these charities. It is important to help the people and the forests.

Try this

Try raising money in your school for charities that help rain forests and the people living there.

FACT FILE

Area

One-quarter of all the land on Earth is covered by forest. That is around 8,500 million acres (3,442 million hectares). Half of these forests are tropical forests.

Protected land

The Manu National Park in Peru is a protected area at the head (beginning) of the Amazon River. It is one of the largest rain forest national parks in the world. It covers 3.7 million acres (1.5 million hectares). About 1,000 different kinds of birds live there, and 15,000 different kinds of plants. There are probably many more we do not know about.

Deadly frog

The poison arrow frog lives in the rain forests of South America. One tiny drop of poison from its skin can kill a human. Hunters use this poison on their arrows. That is how the frog gets its name.

Giant flower

The rafflesia plant has the largest flower in the world. It can grow to 36in (91cm) tall and weigh as much as 24lb (11kg). It grows in the rain forests of Southeast Asia.

Losing forests

About 42 million acres (17 million hectares) of rain forest disappear each year. This works out at about one soccer field every second.

Websites

www. tropical-forests.com

http://kids.ran.org

http://www. rainforestfoundation. org

GLOSSARY

Amazon One of the biggest rivers in the world, in South America. It mainly flows through Brazil.

Canopy The top layer of a rain forest.

Carbon dioxide One of the gases in the air. It is given off when something burns, but is absorbed by green leaves on plants.

Cash crops Crops people grow to sell.

Climate The weather a place gets over a long period of time.

Conifers Trees, such as fir trees and pine trees, which keep their leaves all year round.

Eco-tourism Tourism where visitors learn about living things and the environment.

Equator An imaginary line around the middle of the Earth.

Evaporate To change from a liquid into a gas.

Extinct When an animal or plant dies out.

Fungi Tiny living things that make mushrooms and toadstools.

Global warming The way the climate of the Earth is getting warmer.

Gulley A deep crack in a hillside, often made by water washing the soil away.

Hardwood Strong, heavy wood.

Lichen A kind of plant that grows over stones and on tree trunks.

Logging Cutting down trees for timber.

National park Land protected by a government.

Nature reserve A place where wildlife is safe.

Oxygen One of the main gases in the air.

Most living things need oxygen to survive.

Pollution Poison or other harmful things that get into the environment.

Sustainable forest A forest that is managed by people so that there are always enough trees for the forest to survive.

Temperate Parts of the world that have mild summers and cold winters.

Timber Wood we use in building.

Tropical To do with the Tropics—the areas of the world around the equator. The climate is usually warm here.

Understory The middle layer in a rain forest, beneath the canopy and above the forest floor.

Water vapor Water that has been warmed and become a gas.

INDEX